IF YOU YOU GIVE A GUY A BEER

PHIL NEWTON & J. EDWARD   ILLUSTRATED BY WILLIAM ADAMS

Text Copyright © 2013 by Phil Newton and J. Edward
Illustrations Copyright © 2013 by William Adams
All rights reserved.
ISBN-10: 0615927513
ISBN-13: 978-0615927510 (If You Give A Guy Publications)

If you give a guy a beer,

He'll want popcorn to go with it.

When he gets the popcorn,
he might spill it all over his recliner.

When he reaches into the cushion to dig out the popcorn,
he'll find the $10 bill he lost last year.

Then he'll go to the store to buy more beer.

At the store he'll run into his old high school buddies,
the ones that never grew up.
Seeing them will make him nostalgic.

He'll want to join them,
so he'll jump into their truck and head for a bar...

A bar located in a mobile home.

At the bar he'll run into his old girlfriend.
He'll say, "I'm thankful the fatty dumped me all those years ago."
He'll actually say *those words* out loud.

Then he'll have to fight her brothers.

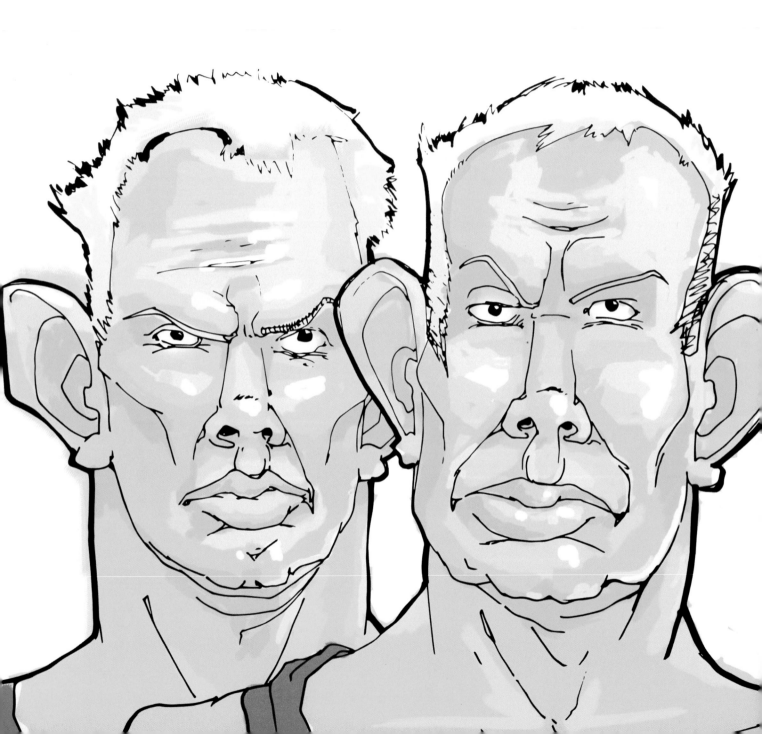

Lucky for him, his friends will "have his back".

Seeing him soaked with beer and beat up will remind everyone of old times...of drinking, playing pool, singing karaoke, and line dancing.

They'll drink, play pool, sing karaoke, and line dance until 3 a.m.,

At which point they'll quickly decide to leave.

His quick exit will remind him of the days when he ran track and field.
He'll jump fences, sprint through cow pastures, and head for the trees.

After wandering through the woods
he'll eventually find his back deck.

At which point it will begin to rain.

Seeing his house, he'll remember how comfortable his recliner is and he'll want to go relax...if only he had his keys.

He'll climb carefully through the window, step on the dog's tail, and bang his shin on the coffee table.

He'll find his recliner,
but his aches and pains will start to catch up with him.

Feeling his aches and pains will remind him of his adventurous night and the beer stuffed in his pants pocket. He'll open the beer and take a sip.

He'll want some popcorn to go with it.

Made in the USA
Las Vegas, NV
06 December 2020